A

Very

Useful

XMAS

PLANNER

Jayme | Books
DESIGN

A BIG THANK YOU

for supporting independant
publishing. We hope you are
happy with your purchase.

In need of a journal, diary or planner?
Be sure to checkout our extensive catalogue
for all manner and type of useful publications.
Everything from financial ledgers, nutritional
planners to coin collecting and even Scuba Diving.
Yes we're that extensive!

We've also a great range of picture and activity
books perfect as children and family gifts
for all occasions we regularly publish
So, be sure to look up the name
next time your on Amazon

REVIEWS ARE IMPORTANT!

Your feedback and comments are greatly appreciated
on Facebook and Amazon. Both help us bring the best to you
and our customers. A few seconds of your precious time would
mean a huge difference to helping us maintain quality
standards. Thank you!

While there why not sign up for our <u>ONCE A MONTH NO SPAM</u>
Newsletter for all latest releases and recommendations

Consider this planner your handy go to guide in helping plan all your important Christmas stuff

Within these pages you can organise and destress with ease

Whether you celebrate big or small, we've got you covered

MAKE HAPPY PLANNING
A HAPPY CHRISTMAS

My 25 Day Count Down Planner

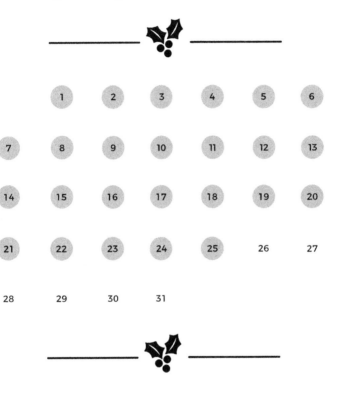

Day 1

_____

Day 2

_____

Day 3

Day 4

Day 5

Day 6

Day 7

Day 8

Day 9

Day 10

Day 11

Day 12

Day 13

Day 14

Day 15

Day 16

Day 16

Day 18

Day 19

Day 20

Day 21

Day 22

Day 23

Day 24

Day 25

Christmas

Wishlist

CHRISTMAS
Wish List

_____

_____

_____

_____

_____

_____

CHRISTMAS
Wish List

_____

_____

_____

_____

_____

CHRISTMAS
Wish List

_____

_____

_____

_____

_____

_____

CHRISTMAS
Wish List

_____

_____

_____

_____

_____

_____

CHRISTMAS
Budget Planner

Date:	Item:	Price:

CHRISTMAS
Budget Planner

Date:	Item:	Price:

# CHRISTMAS
Budget Planner

Date:	Item:	Price:

CHRISTMAS
Budget Planner

Date:	Item:	Price:

Christmas

Gift List

CHRISTMAS
Gift List

Person: Budget: Cost: Bought: ○

                                           Wrapped: ○

Presents: Shop/Website: Posted: ○

Person: Budget: Cost: Bought: ○

                                           Wrapped: ○

Presents: Shop/Website: Posted: ○

Person: Budget: Cost: Bought: ○

                                           Wrapped: ○

Presents: Shop/Website: Posted: ○

Person: Budget: Cost: Bought: ○

                                           Wrapped: ○

Presents: Shop/Website: Posted: ○

Person: Budget: Cost: Bought: ○

                                           Wrapped: ○

Presents: Shop/Website: Posted: ○

CHRISTMAS
Gift List

Person: Budget: Cost: Bought: ⚪

Wrapped: ⚪

Presents: Shop/Website: Posted: ⚪

Person: Budget: Cost: Bought: ⚪

Wrapped: ⚪

Presents: Shop/Website: Posted: ⚪

Person: Budget: Cost: Bought: ⚪

Wrapped: ⚪

Presents: Shop/Website: Posted: ⚪

Person: Budget: Cost: Bought: ⚪

Wrapped: ⚪

Presents: Shop/Website: Posted: ⚪

Person: Budget: Cost: Bought: ⚪

Wrapped: ⚪

Presents: Shop/Website: Posted: ⚪

CHRISTMAS
Gift List

Person: Budget: Cost: Bought: ◯

                                                       Wrapped: ◯

Presents: Shop/Website: Posted: ◯

Person: Budget: Cost: Bought: ◯

                                                       Wrapped: ◯

Presents: Shop/Website: Posted: ◯

Person: Budget: Cost: Bought: ◯

                                                       Wrapped: ◯

Presents: Shop/Website: Posted: ◯

Person: Budget: Cost: Bought: ◯

                                                       Wrapped: ◯

Presents: Shop/Website: Posted: ◯

Person: Budget: Cost: Bought: ◯

                                                       Wrapped: ◯

Presents: Shop/Website: Posted: ◯

CHRISTMAS

Gift List

Person: **Budget:**   **Cost:**   Bought: ○

Wrapped: ○

Presents: **Shop/Website:**   Posted: ○

Person: **Budget:**   **Cost:**   Bought: ○

Wrapped: ○

Presents: **Shop/Website:**   Posted: ○

Person: **Budget:**   **Cost:**   Bought: ○

Wrapped: ○

Presents: **Shop/Website:**   Posted: ○

Person: **Budget:**   **Cost:**   Bought: ○

Wrapped: ○

Presents: **Shop/Website:**   Posted: ○

Person: **Budget:**   **Cost:**   Bought: ○

Wrapped: ○

Presents: **Shop/Website:**   Posted: ○

CHRISTMAS
Gift List

Person: Budget: Cost: Bought: ○

                                                            Wrapped: ○

Presents: Shop/Website: Posted: ○

Person: Budget: Cost: Bought: ○

                                                            Wrapped: ○

Presents: Shop/Website: Posted: ○

Person: Budget: Cost: Bought: ○

                                                            Wrapped: ○

Presents: Shop/Website: Posted: ○

Person: Budget: Cost: Bought: ○

                                                            Wrapped: ○

Presents: Shop/Website: Posted: ○

Person: Budget: Cost: Bought: ○

                                                            Wrapped: ○

Presents: Shop/Website: Posted: ○

CHRISTMAS
Gift List

Person: Budget: Cost: Bought: ○

                                                     Wrapped: ○
Presents: Shop/Website:
                                                     Posted: ○

Person: Budget: Cost: Bought: ○

                                                     Wrapped: ○
Presents: Shop/Website:
                                                     Posted: ○

Person: Budget: Cost: Bought: ○

                                                     Wrapped: ○
Presents: Shop/Website:
                                                     Posted: ○

Person: Budget: Cost: Bought: ○

                                                     Wrapped: ○
Presents: Shop/Website:
                                                     Posted: ○

Person: Budget: Cost: Bought: ○

                                                     Wrapped: ○
Presents: Shop/Website:
                                                     Posted: ○

Christmas
Card List

CHRISTMAS
Card List

Person /Family:

Address:

Posted: ○

Person /Family:

Address:

Posted: ○

Person /Family:

Address:

Posted: ○

Person /Family:

Address:

Posted: ○

Person /Family:

Address:

Posted: ○

CHRISTMAS
Card List

Person /Family:

Address:

Posted: ⭕

Person /Family:

Address:

Posted: ⭕

Person /Family:

Address:

Posted: ⭕

Person /Family:

Address:

Posted: ⭕

Person /Family:

Address:

Posted: ⭕

CHRISTMAS
Card List

Person /Family:

Address:

Posted: ○

Person /Family:

Address:

Posted: ○

Person /Family:

Address:

Posted: ○

Person /Family:

Address:

Posted: ○

Person /Family:

Address:

Posted: ○

CHRISTMAS
Card List

Person /Family:

Address:

Posted: ○

Person /Family:

Address:

Posted: ○

Person /Family:

Address:

Posted: ○

Person /Family:

Address:

Posted: ○

Person /Family:

Address:

Posted: ○

CHRISTMAS

Card List

Person /Family:

Address:

Posted: ○

Person /Family:

Address:

Posted: ○

Person /Family:

Address:

Posted: ○

Person /Family:

Address:

Posted: ○

Person /Family:

Address:

Posted: ○

CHRISTMAS
Card List

Person /Family:

Address:

Posted: ○

Person /Family:

Address:

Posted: ○

Person /Family:

Address:

Posted: ○

Person /Family:

Address:

Posted: ○

Person /Family:

Address:

Posted: ○

Christmas
Shopping List

CHRISTMAS
Shopping List

Shops /Website: **Cost:**   ◯

Presents:

Shops /Website: **Cost:**   ◯

Presents:

Shops /Website: **Cost:**   ◯

Presents:

Shops /Website: **Cost:**   ◯

Presents:

Shops /Website: **Cost:**   ◯

Presents:

CHRISTMAS
Shopping List

Shops /Website:　　　**Cost:**　　　○

Presents:

Shops /Website:　　　**Cost:**　　　○

Presents:

Shops /Website:　　　**Cost:**　　　○

Presents:

Shops /Website:　　　**Cost:**　　　○

Presents:

Shops /Website:　　　**Cost:**　　　○

Presents:

CHRISTMAS
Shopping List

Shops /Website: Cost: ○

Presents:

Shops /Website: Cost: ○

Presents:

Shops /Website: Cost: ○

Presents:

Shops /Website: Cost: ○

Presents:

Shops /Website: Cost: ○

Presents:

CHRISTMAS
Shopping List

Shops /Website:　　　　**Cost:**　　　　○

Presents:

Shops /Website:　　　　**Cost:**　　　　○

Presents:

Shops /Website:　　　　**Cost:**　　　　○

Presents:

Shops /Website:　　　　**Cost:**　　　　○

Presents:

Shops /Website:　　　　**Cost:**　　　　○

Presents:

CHRISTMAS
Shopping List

Shops /Website:　　　　　**Cost:**　　　　　○

Presents:

Shops /Website:　　　　　**Cost:**　　　　　○

Presents:

Shops /Website:　　　　　**Cost:**　　　　　○

Presents:

Shops /Website:　　　　　**Cost:**　　　　　○

Presents:

Shops /Website:　　　　　**Cost:**　　　　　○

Presents:

CHRISTMAS
Shopping List

Shops /Website: **Cost:**   ◯

Presents:

Shops /Website: **Cost:**   ◯

Presents:

Shops /Website: **Cost:**   ◯

Presents:

Shops /Website: **Cost:**   ◯

Presents:

Shops /Website: **Cost:**   ◯

Presents:

CHRISTMAS
Online Order Tracker

Date: Tracking No:

Items: Arrived   ◯

Date: Tracking No:

Items: Arrived   ◯

Date: Tracking No:

Items: Arrived   ◯

Date: Tracking No:

Items: Arrived   ◯

Date: Tracking No:

Items: Arrived   ◯

CHRISTMAS
Online Order Tracker

Date: Tracking No:

Items: Arrived   ◯

Date: Tracking No:

Items: Arrived   ◯

Date: Tracking No:

Items: Arrived   ◯

Date: Tracking No:

Items: Arrived   ◯

Date: Tracking No:

Items: Arrived   ◯

CHRISTMAS
Online Order Tracker

Date: Tracking No:

Items: Arrived   ○

Date: Tracking No:

Items: Arrived   ○

Date: Tracking No:

Items: Arrived   ○

Date: Tracking No:

Items: Arrived   ○

Date: Tracking No:

Items: Arrived   ○

CHRISTMAS
Online Order Tracker

Date: **Tracking No:**

Items: **Arrived** ○

Date: **Tracking No:**

Items: **Arrived** ○

Date: **Tracking No:**

Items: **Arrived** ○

Date: **Tracking No:**

Items: **Arrived** ○

Date: **Tracking No:**

Items: **Arrived** ○

CHRISTMAS
Online Order Tracker

Date: Tracking No:

Items: Arrived ○

Date: Tracking No:

Items: Arrived ○

Date: Tracking No:

Items: Arrived ○

Date: Tracking No:

Items: Arrived ○

Date: Tracking No:

Items: Arrived ○

CHRISTMAS
Online Order Tracker

Date:

Items:

Tracking No:

Arrived ◯

Date:

Items:

Tracking No:

Arrived ◯

Date:

Items:

Tracking No:

Arrived ◯

Date:

Items:

Tracking No:

Arrived ◯

Date:

Items:

Tracking No:

Arrived ◯

CHRISTMAS
Meal Planner

Snacks and
Appetizers:

Dinner:

Deserts and Afters:

Christmas

Recipes

CHRISTMAS
Recipes

Ingrediants

Instructions:

CHRISTMAS
Recipes

Ingrediants

Instructions:

CHRISTMAS
Recipes

Ingrediants

Instructions:

CHRISTMAS
Recipes

Ingrediants

Instructions:

Notes

For next year

NOTES
for Next Year

_____

_____

_____

_____

_____

_____

_____

_____

_____

_____

_____

_____

NOTES

for Next Year

Christmas

Memories

Christmas
 Favourite Memories

_____

_____

_____

_____

_____

_____

_____

_____

_____

_____

_____

.

Printed in Great Britain
by Amazon

35255021R00046